Rock The Bottom

ANDRÉA VAWDA

This book and the successes contained within its pages are made possible through the love, support and patience of my mother.

Table of Contents

Rock The Bottom

Introduction

Maybe I should kill myself. Here I am face down in the dirt. Nothing but gravel and rock everywhere. Deafening silence all around. Gasping for air. Lying on a precipice with cliffs ahead and to each side. No way, no how, no out except to die either by moving and falling off one of the cliffs or by staying still and starving to death.

Okay so I wasn't hanging off a precipice in real life, but circumstances led me to a place where I thought there was no way out except to end it all. After many years of counseling others to deal with their life circumstances, somehow, I was unable to deal with my own except to quit life. I researched methods to find the one that would be the least painful but most effective and discovered a website that rated the agony level of various methods. That agony chart made me press the pause button and rethink my plan.

Hitting rock bottom can be the most significant, impactful, and, yet, devastating experience that a human being can endure. However don't worry, you don't have to have hit a rock bottom that results in the contemplation of suicide to be able to use the offerings contained in this book. Any low point in your life can be an experience that is transformational if you are open to letting that happen. So how do we open to the transformational benefits and insights of rock bottom?

You've already begun to open yourself to those benefits and insights by just opening the pages or downloading the book. Through the years, I coached many people as they navigated their way through their rock bottom by giving them coping strategies and multi-step care plans. The humbling reality I experienced when I hit my own rock bottom is that multi-step care plans rather than being helpful are daunting and defeating. Moving out of rock bottom only needs to be done in very small increments and doesn't have to be complicated or weighty.

When I first started writing this book, I thought that this would be my testimony, my gift to help others to be healed. Then, as time passed, I realized that healing is not a journey to a singular state or destination. Healing is a state of constant openness and regardless of where we are when we start on that journey, we are all on a path of continual improvement and awareness. So that changed my purpose for this book. I am putting it out into the world in partnership, friendship, and collaboration with you as you move through your current temporary darkness and for us to use as a DIY guide for the journey we are both on.

I truly believe that rock bottom can be one of the most transformational destinations that any of us experience. So how can we open to the lessons of Rock Bottom without causing any further damage in our lives? How can we open to the power of Rock Bottom to experience mental and emotional transformations? I slowly learned how to Rock the Bottom. None of this will be shared from a place of telling you what YOU should do - rather it will be sharing my story so that it will be here whenever you decide that you want to hear it.

So, for whatever reason you decided to pick up a book called Rock the Bottom, I believe you were meant to be reading this. Your story may be like mine or it may be different. I hope that as you read this book the similarities of our growth will be more striking than the similarities of our most trying moments.

We each have our own agency and sovereignty and I bring this book to you as my personal journey. Your journey will be unique to you. This book is intended to be a guide not a prescription - it is my unique story. I do not consider myself as an expert in anything. As you read the book, please take from it the things that work for you in your life and leave the rest.

Rock The Bottom

Rock The Bottom

Chapter One

"The only difference between stumbling blocks and steppingstones is how you use them." American Proverb

My journey started in 2017 when I suffered a major health crisis while I was at work. It started as a day like any other day although I had been feeling unwell for several months. Looking back, I realize I was feeling unwell for years. Slowly, slowly pain had become my new normal. I reached a point where I was ignoring the signs from my body that something was genuinely wrong. That day it all finally caught up with me.

I collapsed at work. That's not strictly true...I left work and staggered down what seemed to be an endless sidewalk to where my car was parked on the street. Once there I collapsed. Even though I realized I was in real trouble I found myself debating whether I needed to ask for help. Finally, after vomiting repeatedly and losing my vision, I called my Mum. She arrived a very short time later and immediately called an ambulance and before I knew it, I was in the emergency room of the hospital.

Following several tests in the ER, it was

determined that I had suffered a stroke and I was admitted to the stroke ward at the hospital. Because of my relatively young age, the doctors ordered more than a week of tests to determine what had caused the stroke. Finally, they had an answer - a rare tumor called a myxoma was found in the left atrium of my heart.

This lemon-sized tumor had been throwing off small clots into my bloodstream which had caused small transient ischemic attacks known as TIA's or mini-strokes that had been diagnosed as migraine headaches for years. Knowing now that this is what had been happening to me over the years was very frightening. And having just experienced a larger stroke made me terrified of what could happen next.

What did all of this mean for the state of my brain, my health and my future? At this moment of fear and confusion, I was a long way from seeing this crisis for what it was - an invitation to open. This wasn't my first invitation to open, neither would it be my last but at that time it was certainly the loudest.

I underwent a successful 4-hour open-heart surgery to remove the tumor. The healing process from that surgery through the months that followed gave me my first real insight into the process of healing. The physical healing progressed well - even the previously ever-present migraines disappeared - and because of that, I thought all was well. I returned to work, did the cardiac rehab, and resumed the rest of the regular doings of my life. However, slowly over the following months, I felt out of touch with myself. Ill at ease. Uncomfortable within. All was well with my physical health so what was going on with my emotional/mental/spiritual health?

As I continued to move through my regular life in the months that followed, I could feel that something was holding me back from achieving even the smallest milestones that I set for myself.

As I turned my attention and focus to trying to understand what was happening, it became clear to me that at least part of the struggle was between the version of myself that was a victim and the version of myself that knew itself to be a victor. A victim - what? Impossible! Wasn't I the person who had dragged myself to my car while in the middle of a stroke just so that I wouldn't be a burden on anyone? How is that person a victim? But there it was - the truth staring at me. Although I had intellectually labeled myself as strong, resilient, independent, and fearless the emotional side of me had defined me as a victim that needed to be rescued. And that was where I was living.

The process I was going through didn't match anything that I had ever read about in a book or seen on a screen. That awareness was the first time I thought I should write about my experience because surely, I couldn't be the only one who didn't see themselves reflected in other people's stories. So as I continue to share my story with you, I will also share with you, not strategies or processes, but instead, the openness that I came to understand is necessary to be able to grow, heal and thrive. I know I've mentioned being open a few times now - I promise I will explain what I mean.

Chapter Two

"When you complain you make yourself a victim. Leave the situation, change the situation or accept it, all else is madness." Eckhart Tolle

Why does it seem sometimes easier for us to think of ourselves as the victim? This is not a comfortable truth but in certain situations, we are happy to trade our power and our strength for the comfort of having other people take over and rescue us when we call on them. Only you can determine whether you are a victim of circumstance or whether the truth deep inside you is that you may be a voluntary victim. A voluntary victim chooses and feels a strong identification with the role of the victim in their life.

The Stoics have a great attitude to suffering and they say that all suffering would be ended if we only focused on the things within our control. When we define ourselves as a victim, what we are saying is that something outside of our control has impacted us so deeply and so fully that it has changed our entire inner being. That the situation or event or person has completely transformed the path of our lives and there is nothing that we can do about it.

Is that true?

Think for a second about the weight of the word victim. It's a word that carries a heaviness and sadness and darkness. And, in many cases, the heaviness, sadness and darkness reflect the truth of the circumstances that brought us to this place of feeling helpless and hopeless. It takes time to heal and transition from that emotional state of being. Time to slowly reframe from victim to survivor and then to the victor. And it is important to know that no matter how bad we feel, how helpless we feel or how hopeless we feel, reframing is possible for all of us - it is how we take back control.

Sometimes it's easier to stay in a sad, dark place. Sometimes there is comfort in that sadness and darkness. It becomes a familiar place for us. It becomes a way of operating in the world. Trust me, I get it - I do. I spent a lot of time there and I created a picture of myself in that place that I hung on the walls of every corridor that I walked down in life. It was only when I began to explore the inner parts of myself that I recognized questions that I had never thought to ask of myself - how did I get here and how can I get out?

Remember that picture I talked about in the Introduction about me lying face down in the gravel believing there was no way out? The truth is that the journey from victim to victor can begin with the tiniest of steps and the smallest of actions. If we allow ourselves to be open to something different, I don't mean open to a step-by-step plan, I mean open to possibility however small that things could be different.

When our faces are buried in what we can't control - in this case, the gravel - if we open ourselves to the possibility that something could be different even just easing into a temporary state of openness we see that it would be so much easier to breathe if we just lifted our head enough to turn it to the side.

By looking in a new direction we open ourselves up to a new possibility, one that may help transform our situation. Breathing more easily may only be a 2% change but that small thing means my situation would be 2% different and maybe 2% better. And that's a beginning. Because as we then transition into that space where the 2% gain is, we will find another 2% and another 2%, and then we slowly start to dig our way out using each 2% perspective shift as a foothold.

Throughout my early trials with my health, I always looked for the quick fix, a silver bullet. It was always someone else's job to heal me – whether it was the medical system, internet searches or prescriptions. My constant perspective was that I didn't ask for this, I didn't deserve this, and somebody or something needed to be found to fix me. I did need professionals for some aspects of the "fixing" process – the diagnosis, the surgery and the rehabilitation. Those doctors and physiotherapists were essential. But as I said earlier the physical healing from the surgery was going well. It was the emotional/mental/spiritual healing that wasn't keeping pace. I felt outside of myself.

Disconnected from my body in a way I found difficult to define. Who could fix that for me? Where could I go to get the cure for that? To reconnect with my body, I decided to get a tattoo at the base of my skull where the stroke had happened. I thought it would be a way of honoring the trauma of the day of the stroke and that the physical nature of the tattoo gun might shock my mind into reconnecting with my body. That didn't work. So I started to see a therapist 6 months after the surgery in the hope that she would be able to provide me with answers and a cure.

There was no cure, but she did explain the disconnection I was feeling. She helped me to understand that it was my mind's response to the trauma of the stroke, the fear and the surgery. Now that I had an explanation of this strange feeling it just added to my sense of why me? I didn't see anyone else going through this. Yet another thing over which I had no control. Just great! Inside I was angry and sad and confused and so uneasy. On the outside I was playing what I thought of as my ordained role of "survivor" and everyone around me confirmed me in that role. These two ways of being were impossible for me to reconcile but I kept trying.

Over the next ten months, I made several attempts to bring happiness into my life. I went on a trip to Bali with a friend, I bought a new-to-me car and began a new relationship. To go on the trip I had to get a series of vaccinations which made me feel unwell for a while. The trip was interesting but stressful. When I got home from the trip, I had the first of a new type of migraine that frightened me, and they lasted for just over 3 months. When they ended, a deep fatigue came over me.

The new-to-me car was a big expense which was stressful and although it is a nice car it did not bring the long-lasting happiness, I expected it would. The new relationship was with a man who was very different from the usual type of person I found attractive. It progressed very quickly, burned out, and came to a very sudden and emotional end. These external things were not the fix for the internal problem I was experiencing. Even the therapist couldn't reach it.

Chapter Three

"When we are no longer able to change a situation, we are challenged to change ourselves." Viktor Frankl

There's a well-known story about interference with a caterpillar going through the transformation to become a butterfly. To do that it first creates a cocoon and then transforms into a butterfly which must struggle to escape from that cocoon. Watching this process it appears that the butterfly inside the cocoon is stuck and struggling for its very life. And that's exactly what is happening – the butterfly is struggling to survive. The story is that someone, upon seeing this, decided to cut a very small slit in the sack of the cocoon so that the butterfly could breathe more easily. What happened, however, is that the butterfly fell out of the cocoon, was unable to fly, and fell to the ground where it died. The struggle to breathe and to break out of the cocoon is exactly how the butterfly's wings are strengthened and it can fly.

Strength always must come from within – nobody can give you your strength. Nobody can give you strong biceps by doing your push-ups or pull-ups for you. It's the same with emotional and spiritual strength. Strength can only come through your efforts. Having people support you along the way is a blessing as you go through the process. But make no mistake, the process itself must come from within. You must strengthen your mind and spirit in the same way the butterfly strengthened its wings. And by doing that rather than getting the miracle of a new situation you get the miracle of being able to view your current situation differently. Although this is not a religious experience it is very firmly rooted in spiritual growth.

Our strength comes through the struggle. And the struggle is not over for me - it might not be over for you. Almost every day I dreamt some kind person would finally come along and cut me out of my cocoon of pain. Although I don't know what makes up your cocoon and maybe you're not clear on that either, what I do know is that we both have the power within us to escape and fly. How you do that might be different from the blueprint that you had for your life – perhaps you will never return to the "normal" version of your life that you held in your head. So much stress, anxiety and torment are caused by comparing ourselves to a version of a story that we told ourselves at a young age based on our perception of what was going on around us. That story impacts most of our decisions throughout our lives without us even realizing the weight of that impact.

Looking back at my history from childhood, I started to see how I took on the heavy load of what my dad was carrying – inadvertently believing that I, a young child, could help him. My father was a very complicated man. On the one hand, he was a man with a very generous heart toward others, and on the other hand, he carried a story of hurt that manifested as anger, rage, and violence in his life. It consumed him so much that it eventually defined him. The rage and anger blinded him to the effects that they had on the people around him. As a child, I inadvertently internalized those intense emotions. I carried his negativity inside of me for many, many years and it wasn't until much later that I realized just what a toxic effect it was having on my life. From childhood to adulthood I tried to heal my father without success. I took on that same responsibility with the other male figures in my life and was equally unsuccessful with them. It took me a long time to begin to understand that the only person I could heal was me.

My health issues would mirror those of my father to a frightening extent – he had so much internalized negative emotion that he developed digestive issues. Those same issues began to plague me from the age of 11. His constant migraines were something I began to experience from the age of 13. Later in life, he had problems with his heart which, as I've told you, I would later find out I also had. None of this was evident to me at the time - it is only by looking backward that I can see the effects that this generational trauma had on me. Ultimately those effects brought me to the point of attempted suicide.

On top of the health issues that I had amassed over the years, I had also managed to develop and carry with me this unmanageable level of fear. During one of my classes at university, I watched a documentary that explained how most of the population lives paycheck to paycheck and is only one illness away from poverty which could mean they were just one step away from homelessness. For some reason, this statistic struck at the very core of my being. It bred great insecurity and I began to live my life in hypervigilance to ensure I could prevent that absolute worst outcome from happening to me. To this day I'm sure that level of stress attacked parts of my nervous system and messed up my stress responses. I know now that psychological trauma repeated daily can lead to physical health symptoms.

What I didn't know then was the magnitude of

the health conditions that were building inside me.

I managed the digestive distress for more than 30 years by using and abusing various over-the-counter remedies. The migraines for many years were a monthly event and I managed them by "pushing through" and using non-prescription pain medications. Then they suddenly became an every-other-day event. I continued to "push through" and use the same pain medications but also started to seek medical help. Over the next 3 years, I met with many neuro-specialists, and I was repeatedly tested, poked and prodded. None of them had the answer.

The medical answer to the migraines came following the fateful day of the stroke. However, the emotional/spiritual answer was still more than a year away. I contend that the tumor in my heart was a direct result of the years of carrying unresolved trauma in my spirit. The physical manifestations I experienced were invitations to address and resolve that trauma. Through the years, I was asking entirely the wrong question. I was asking how to make it stop when the right question instead was how to address fear and insecurity.

I'm a firm believer that life will keep giving you invitations until you finally realize what they are and make the decision to accept the invitation. An invitation to what? To look within, to be still, to heal, to absolve, to forgive, to just stop. It can be anything, but it will never be something external. You will never get an invitation to make more money or drive a faster car – sorry about that! But what you can be 100% sure of is that we will continue to receive these invitations until we understand, acknowledge, and accept.

And guess what the best part is? My experience is that every time you ignore an invitation, the next one is bigger and more insistent! So the invitations that came to me started as somewhat small quiet intrusions in my life. Nothing I couldn't ignore or manage. As time went on, they became more frequent and less manageable. However, I did not recognize them for what they were. I was still focusing on carrying the weight and the burdens of everyone in my life and trying to fit into all these roles I believed were expected of me as a daughter, mother, employee and friend. Finally, the stroke was the invitation that got my attention. It was so loud it almost knocked me unconscious.

That invitation would spark a string of events that would see me broken down mentally, physically, emotionally and spiritually. And when I thought it was over and that I was where I needed to be I was hit with an invitation that very nearly ensured that I would never have another chance to get things right.

Rock The Bottom

Chapter Four

"Although the world is full of suffering, it is also full of the overcoming of it." Helen Keller

As the Buddhist quote says "Pain is inevitable. Suffering is optional". How is that possible? Pain is a communication between our body, mind, and spirit that something is requiring our attention. It is an invitation to bring focus to a particular area of our lives or a specific occurrence. For example, the pain of a stroke is communicating that your body needs urgent medical attention; the pain of grief is communicating that your emotional and mental health needs your attention and assistance; spiritual pain is communicating that your relationship with the Divine requires your focus.

There are many tools we can use to offset the pain we experience in our lives. For physical pain from a stroke, the pain can be offset by medical interventions. With emotional and mental pain counseling, medical and self-help therapies can offset that pain. Spiritual pain can be offset through prayer and counseling. Suffering occurs when we choose not to make use of any of the interventions available to us. So we feel immobilized. Living with our unhappiness can often feel like the easiest choice. All change is hard and scary. The outcome is unknown. So we choose to sit in our unhappiness and suffer.

A large part of the pain that we experience at Rock Bottom, is due to the story that we tell ourselves about who we are, what our life is, and what we deserve. There's a saying "Comparison is the thief of joy." Our expectations, the story we create based on what we think we should be, what we think we should be doing, and what we think others think we should be doing creates an unwinnable scenario in our lives.

The most pain many of us experience comes from the awareness that our current reality does not match those expectations. The constant comparison of our reality against the idealistic image we have set up in our minds leads us to the conclusion that we are not enough and that we can never be enough.

Suffering at Rock Bottom is due to our state of paralysis. Because of the constant cycle of comparing what we see as the reality of our lives to what we perceive as the expectations for our lives, we feel unable to move. We don't know how to break that cycle. We are afraid to move forward even though it's painful to stay where we are.

Let's go back to my story of life on the precipice. You'll remember that I had managed to achieve a 2% improvement by turning my head to the side and was now able to breathe better. With the easier breathing, I was free to expand my focus to examine what else was around me on that side. I could see that there was more than just the precipice I was lying on. Looking across the canyon looming below, I could see the horizon way off in the distance.

Okay! So there was the possibility of a place somewhere other than this precipice. When we can increase our awareness of where we are at any moment, it creates space for possibility at that moment. When we make small changes, even very small changes, we can see that something different is a possibility. Even a small 2% change is something different from the paralysis we were experiencing. Each incremental change leads us closer to hope.

One small change that each of us can make in our lives is how we talk to ourselves. Most of us are much harder on ourselves than we are on others. That starts with self-talk. For example, making the change from the word "should" to the word "could" when we talk to ourselves. The statement or thought of "I should go to the gym today" can become "I could go to the gym today". Do you feel the difference between those two sentences?

"Should" sentences in our lives are sentences of implied expectation with some guilt woven into them if we are unable to meet the expectation. Those sentences start from when we are very young. They are sentences spoken by people of authority or assumed authority in our lives - parents, teachers, bosses, talking heads on TV, social media influencers, etc. The implied expectation sets us up with the fear of not being able to meet the expectation. That sets up a cycle of self-talk that can lead us to a point where we may believe we will fall short of success. That can leave us with no motivation to even try which leaves us stuck where we are.

If we use "could" sentences, they open the door to feeling empowered about the thing you "could" be doing. There is a sense of choice. With choice, we feel free to decide how we approach something. We feel less resistant to deciding.

Chapter Five

"You can't connect the dots looking forward." Steve Jobs

Maybe I should kill myself. That thought woke me in the middle of the night ripping me out of sleep. I had fallen asleep on the couch and now here I was alone in the living room in the dark with this very powerful and foreign thought. WTF? What had brought this on? Adrenaline was pumping through me. I didn't feel like myself. As I considered the thought, I did a review of my life to this point and now the thought didn't seem so strange. Maybe it was worth considering.

So for the next couple of hours, that's what I did. I thought about ways I could kill myself. There was a friend who had a gun - I could probably get access to that sometime in the morning. I could use a kitchen knife and stab myself directly in the heart. Maybe I could get some heroin or fentanyl. Although all of these were possibilities, none of them seemed like the right answer. So I went online and searched for methods of suicide. I landed on a site that provided various methods and had an "agony scale".

This scale measured the level of pain that

would be experienced with each method. I looked at all the different ways of getting the job done and ultimately settled on asphyxiation by hanging. It had worked for Kate Spade and Robin Williams. Once I had settled on the method, I felt calmer and went to bed and slept.

When I woke in the morning, I looked back on the night and dismissed it as "middle of the night insanity". I recognized though that I was feeling very emotionally low and that my physical energy was also low. I was on vacation leave that week, so I reached out to my mother, and we met to do some shopping. As we walked through the store, I felt myself getting more and more physically tired and I felt disoriented. At the same time, my right eye began to bother me. Gradually over that day the pain in my eye grew and started to take up my complete focus. My vacation leave was over at the end of that week, and I returned to work. By that time both eyes had become extremely painful and nothing I did seemed to provide relief - I used warm compresses, cold compresses, and various types of eye drops but nothing worked. As the next couple of weeks progressed that pain drove out everything else in my life.

Within a couple of days of returning to work, I was unable to focus past the pain. I met with my regular optometrist who referred me to a specialty optometrist to see if they could provide me with some relief. They didn't have the answer. After several more weeks of this type of pain without respite, I returned to what I saw as the only solution to the problem ... ending my life. I planned and did a trial run.

Knowing that there was a solution that I could implement whenever I chose gave me at least a temporary sense of relief. As the weeks progressed, the pain continued to be unrelenting. Finally, on a Saturday night with my teenage daughter in the other room, I decided I couldn't go on any longer. I set myself up and just as I was beginning to asphyxiate myself my daughter called through my closed door to me to tell me my mother was on the phone for me. I hesitated but then took her call. As we talked, I told her how desperate I was and that I didn't think I could live with this type of pain for much longer.

Fortunately, I had a previously scheduled counseling appointment on Monday. Following that appointment during which I told my counselor about the point of desperation I had reached over the weekend; I went to the emergency ward of my local general hospital. I was treated there by a psychiatrist who suggested I should admit myself for a couple of days unless I was able to stay with someone. My daughter would be staying with her father that week and I went to stay with my mother. That arrangement lasted for the next two months. Those 2 months were the beginning of my journey of 2% changes.

We have so many choices and freedoms in our lives and one of the biggest choices we have is to choose freedom from suffering. None of us get to choose whether we will experience pain. Unfortunately, that is a fact of life - at some point we all experience pain. It can be physical, emotional, or spiritual.

However, we do not need to suffer because of the pain. We can choose what to do with the pain. Do we try to make even that 2% change to begin the transition from pain to healing or do we instead begin the transition from pain to suffering by giving up? The moment you decide to make ANY kind of change, healing begins.

Think of it this way - we are all born with a battery full of power. Then through conditioning and suffering, clinging and resisting we begin to lose some of that power. I have found myself many times through the years grappling with a reduced battery. The good news is that we can recharge. It has been my experience that we can regain our power 2% at a time. No matter our circumstances, a 2% change is something we can all do. Regaining our power doesn't need to be complicated or painful.

We look at "hopeful" as a future tense word. If hope is "a feeling or inspiring optimism about a future event" what if we bring "hope" and "hopeful" into our present experience? It's more than acceptance or surrender. It is feeling inspired within the moment. It's trusting that your dots are all connecting in the present even though you can't see it at the time.

I was chatting with a friend one Friday. He was expressing his impatience for the workday ahead in great anticipation of the weekend. I sympathized and reassured him the day would be through soon enough. It was in this moment of mindless comfort that I came to terms with an integral part of bringing hope into the present moment.

The common complaint of 9-to-5ers is that the weekends go by too quickly. How can we make the weekends last longer? they often debate. I've certainly felt that way too. This is a very relatable example for all of us that when we spend our work week wishing each day away, we focus our attention on the reality that time is worth wishing away. Throughout the workweek, we project to our weekend days off and when we finally get there those 2 days go by so quickly.

We know that energy flows where our attention goes. So should it be a surprise that after spending the previous 5 days wishing that minutes and hours would speed up that those same minutes and hours on a weekend disappear so quickly?

I've spent so much of my life wishing away the present in hopes of a better future. This created a present that felt like something from which I needed to escape. So I lived in a continuous state of projecting to a conjured and fictitious future. This made my present even more unbearable to live in because it could never match up to that luminous future. And so I would continue the projection and the cycle.

Going back now to my story of life on the precipice we left me with a new awareness that there was something beyond the precipice. So if there was something on that side of the precipice maybe there was something on the other side as well. I had made a 2% shift and that began to change my present reality. By changing that 2% in the present causes our future to shift too. So if our future is the result of all the things that came before, imagine how transformational that can be! It means this very moment wherever you are is just the residual of what you've been previously thinking and doing. By choosing to be "awake" in this present moment by embracing hope, not as a future aspiration, opens the door for the next present moment to be something different. Something we are not wishing away.

And I get it - maybe the circumstances in the next present moment will still suck. I've been there! My circumstances as I said earlier left me feeling I thought the only way to deal was to escape by ending my life. But if you continue to stay "awake" I can promise that the circumstances in the next present moment and the next after that and the one after that will be different than they were before you "woke up".

Rock The Bottom

Chapter Six

"It is your reaction to adversity, not the adversity itself, that determines how your life story will develop." Dieter F. Uchtdorf

For the first few weeks of those next 2 months, I lived a very regimented existence. It was the only way I could tolerate being awake. The pain of my eyes was intolerable and there was no way to escape from it while I was awake. I spent many, many hours lying down with an ice mask over my eyes and dispensed liters of eye drops into my eyes. I was alone with my thoughts and had no way to distract myself from them. I couldn't watch any screens, I couldn't read a book, I couldn't bear to have my eyes open for more than 5-10 minutes at a time. I was so agitated all the time.

I recognized that I needed to find a way to calm myself. I figured out a way to change the settings on my phone to accommodate my eyes for a few minutes at a time. So I started looking up meditations. This was something very new to me. It was not who I thought I was. I stumbled around YouTube looking for something that would help me to settle myself. I found a guided meditation that talked about self-healing. Finally, something that was giving me a focus! This meditation talked about how our cells know what they are doing; that our health is our birthright and that we can help our cells through the creation of positive emotions and stress reduction. When I heard this there was a deeper knowing that came over me or maybe I just felt comforted by it. I listened to that meditation over and over and over. It was a great distraction from the pain and discomfort.

I began to look for other meditations that were talking about this same reality and I was amazed at how many there were! Never in my life had I been so desperate for answers; never in my life had I been so open to everything. The resolution of the strokes and TIA's I had suffered was achieved with the removal of the tumor in my heart. That had been a quick and permanent resolution to my health issues. Although I experienced discomfort during the physical healing period afterward, I was following a known plan moving forward from one step to the next. This situation with my eyes had no such plan. The doctors I was seeing told me there was only modest treatment available which I discovered meant there were no known cures. What?!! I felt abandoned and alone. The idea that this present condition might be a forever thing was terrifying. I refused to believe it. I began to look everywhere for answers. Meanwhile, things seemed to get worse.

I was in a state of unrest, panic, and desperation. One night as I was listening to yet another guided meditation something happened. The meditation directed me to reflect on a recent difficult time when I needed support. I recalled an incident a few days earlier when I was lying down in the bottom of my bathtub with the water from the showerhead running over my body. I had no energy to move, no desire to do anything except to lie there in the misery and powerlessness I was experiencing. Why me? Why now?

The meditation directed me to go to myself in that situation and hold myself. Seriously? This was a real stretch for me. However, because I was so desperate for an answer, I was willing to try anything. I pictured myself standing over me in the tub and I reached down and lifted my naked, wet body up and out of the tub. Then I cuddled myself to my chest the way a mother holds a small child. That was the most amazing feeling I had ever experienced. The holding and the being held all at the same time. I carried myself into my bedroom and tucked myself into bed, stroked my forehead, and then sat beside the bed. I reached out to myself in the bed and promised that I would remain by the bed and watch over me and that I would figure out how to heal all that ailed me. I came out of this meditation with tears streaming down my face.

Returning now for a moment to my story of life on the precipice. Suddenly my left leg developed an extremely painful charley horse in the calf. The contractions of my calf muscle were excruciating, and the pain began to extend down into my foot. I screamed in agony and involuntarily stretched my leg. The spasm eased. Relief and gratitude washed over me followed by the awareness that my body had instinctively known what to do to put an end to the paroxysm of pain. Incredible! Not only that but moving my leg had not made me fall off the cliff to my death.

As a result of the reliving and re-authoring of my memory, I realized that I had hit rock bottom and survived. Not only had I survived but I had received G.O.D, also what I refer to as the Gift of Desperation. But being human I began to question that moment almost immediately. I vacillated between sureness of the experience and doubt that the connection was real. The voice of doubt was loud. To counteract it, I tied a piece of ribbon around my wrist as a reminder of my belief in the invitation to connect. I had no idea where to go with this new profound belief that I could heal. I decided that I would have to be willing to consider everything. That's not to say that I haven't continued to struggle with doubt and fear. I still find myself scared in moments because I am still learning how to receive and accept the fullness of this invitation into my life.

Rock The Bottom

Chapter Seven

"The significant problems we have cannot be solved at the same level of thinking with which we created them." Albert Einstein

The term "Gift of Desperation" or "GOD" is a term that is often used in addiction recovery circles. Largely this is because rock bottom is a well-known state of being for this group of people. However, rock bottom can happen to anyone at any time and the desperation that comes with being in that place is common to everybody regardless of the reason for the rock bottom experience. Not everybody receives the Gift of Desperation because they are unable to move past the limitations set by their ego. For our purposes right now, "EGO" is defined as "Edging God Out". Wayne Dyer identifies the following 6 components of EGO –

1. I am what I have. (My possessions define me)
2. I am what I do. (My achievements define me)
3. I am what others think of me. (My reputation defines me)
4. I am separate from everyone. (My body defines me as alone)
5. I am separate from all that is missing in my life.

6. I am separate from God.

None of these statements is true but almost every person, without ever questioning the proof of any of them, believes them to be the truth of life. We judge our success in life based on these statements which means that we can never be on the winning side. Look at just the first 3 of them and you can see that we're already going to be "failing" because someone else will always have acquired more than we have; have achieved more success than we have; be more well-known than we are. Looking at the last 3 statements, we can only feel a failure because they mean our success must be measured on the physical plane and it is simply not possible to completely merge our physical self with others or with things or with God.

These 6 factors are in large part the cause of our fall to rock bottom. When we are living and measuring our lives based on these factors, we are unable to see any other way of being. The Gift of Desperation seems only to become visible once we have landed and spent some time on rock bottom. Self-help books, therapists, Buddhists, the Dalai Lama, and other guru-like people use phrases that include words such as "trust", "accept", "surrender" and "detach". To many of us when we are in a place of desperation these words may seem to be a state of being that is inaccessible and incomprehensible. They may also ignite strong feelings of opposition because they feel pointless. To "trust" meant moving forward blindly in the dark refusing to ask for proof which seemed reckless and careless and a sure-fire way to ensure failure. The old way of doing meant that to "accept" really meant settling. To "surrender" meant to give up which resulted in being stuck in place. To "detach" seemed like a cold cutting off of people or situations in my life which would lead to further isolation. All of these seemed to fuel my victim story.

What I have learned after my time at rock bottom is that moving to a new state of being required no more than a 2% shift in my thinking. What I mean by a new state of being is exactly that - a state of being rather than a state of doing.

My state of doing meant that I was spending my time trying to outrun what was happening to me. It meant that I spent massive amounts of time running toward what I thought would be "cures" for my condition. I ran to my doctors pushing at them to provide the silver bullet that would end all my sufferings. I also ran after every possible idea that appeared in my endless Google searches looking for an answer. I spent months trying to leave my suffering behind.

When I received the Gift of Desperation and began to understand that there was the power of the divine within me and that my body could heal itself, I knew I had to refocus my time and energy to understand how to help my body to do that. I knew that I could not keep going at the pace that I had been. So I slowed down. That slowdown allowed me the time to review my current situation and try to understand how I got there and how to move out of it. As part of that process, I began to realize that I had spent most of my life on the run from one thing or another in a constant state of busyness. And that slowdown was the 2% shift that began the transition from my state of doing to a state of being.

Moving back to my time on the precipice, the surprise I felt that I hadn't fallen over the edge of the cliff when my leg moved led me to consider that my previously held convictions might not be true. Maybe I wasn't stuck here forever. If I could move one leg without falling, maybe I could move my other leg or maybe I could even move my arms and push myself up. Suddenly I felt like there might be a way out that didn't end in my death.

Chapter Eight

"Now that you are willing to understand, you have taken the first step to understand." Bram Stoker

Rock Bottom is an invitation to open - opening up within ourselves; opening up to what is; opening to our present state of being. First, we open a little to the possibility that life circumstances could be different. If we can't reach that then all we need to be is open to the possibility of being open.

You see, it doesn't matter where we step in. The place doesn't matter. Being open is what matters. If we can be even the slightest bit open, then we have already created a little space for something different to occur.

If I lie face down on the precipice wholly convinced that this is all there is then it very well could be all there is for me. Like Henry Ford said, "whether you believe you can or you can't, either way, you'll be right." It's not even about figuring anything out. We can become so overwhelmed trying to sort the details that we feel doomed even to begin. But here's the thing - this isn't a list of complex steps or a strategy to be followed. All that is required is to be a little bit open to something different. And when we are then something different will present itself to us. Like me face down on the precipice and just by opening myself to the possibility that something could be different, I came into the realization that I could turn my head and right away I could breathe more easily. I was just open to possibility which allowed me to understand that there was more than just this one precipice in my life. I continue to welcome a state of being open and now though my body is still on the cliff, I can move it 2% at a time.

When these shifts come into my awareness I do just that - I shift and, in my time, I'm now on my knees and see the world around me very differently than I did when I was face down. I'm beginning to understand that there is nothing wrong with any of us. That the old story that tells us we must remove or rid ourselves of pieces or parts of ourselves to be better just is not true. I believe that practicing openness to possibility is not only the most accessible way to change in our lives but will also be the most powerful. Being open to all my pieces and parts hasn't resulted in the healing I once thought it would, but I have come into the awareness that I don't need healing. I am not broken. I am not lacking. Instead, simply through the course of life conditioning I became distracted from the truth that I am whole inside, and that wellness is already mine.

This awareness only came a bit at a time for me and I resisted it many times or at best could only grasp a small piece at a time. But - yup! you know what's coming - I stayed open to the possibilities and now I feel this truth inside my physical body. And here's the best part! You, too, are magnificent and although it is sometimes difficult to forget about how we have operated in the world in the past, things we have done, or thoughts and feelings we've had, all you need to do to access your true magnificence is to become open to the possibility. By being open, I find myself more frequently in a state of acceptance instead of resistance. I've come to discover that this space allows for the possibilities to come into my reality.

Rock The Bottom

Chapter Nine

"Who you are tomorrow begins with what you do today"
Tim Fargo

Being open was a new concept for me and maybe it is for you too. It didn't mean saying "yes" to everything. but I realized saying "no" to everything didn't seem to be working. So, instead of saying "no" so quickly I started doing my best to be open to any idea that presented itself. I would let the idea percolate in my mind overnight or for a couple of days. What I found was that just the act of letting these ideas in and spending time with them showed me that many of them were pretty good. They made me want to say "yes" to them whereas my first instinct had been to reject them, to say "no". That automatic rejection was simply because it was scary to think about doing something new. So I continued to practice opening myself to the idea of being open. Open to what? I didn't know! But nothing else had worked for me so I had to look at this as a possibility. Then that possibility became a possibility. It all compounded as I continued to practice openness. Gradually things, including actual things, began to present themselves that would inevitably direct my life in a way that I never imagined.

I began to experience my life in a way that was closed to me before. My prior limited reality was broadening and expanding. Then along the way, I read some scientific articles about the electromagnetic frequency spectrum. Along the spectrum, there are microwaves, gamma waves, x-rays, and all kinds of other frequencies including light which is the only frequency that human beings can perceive. It turns out that light makes up only 0.0035% of the spectrum. Think of that for a moment. The light that we as human beings can perceive is far less than one-quarter of one percent of the entire field of the electromagnetic spectrum! That means that more than 99.997% of the spectrum exists and we cannot perceive it! It exists but we cannot see it or touch it.

Think about it this way. We, as human beings devise our lives based on what we can see. Our reality is built on less than a quarter of one percent of what is present in our world. This blew my mind wide open! If I've only been using less than one-quarter of one percent how limited am I? Seriously! I decided to try to be open to the other 99.997%. The stuff I can't see - I know it sounds a bit crazy.

The older version of me would have said I was a nut job. But here's the thing, of the things we can't see one of them is the law of aerodynamics and it was only through the Wright brothers and other open-minded thinkers that planes were built that could use this invisible law. And guess what happened? The miracle of the flight occurred where tons of metal is now able to fly. What seemed impossible became possible - a new reality. When you are open to the possibility you gain access to the 99.997%!! Being open allows space for new thinking and possibilities to unfold.

So going back to me now in a kneeling position on the precipice I choose to move another 2% by rocking back onto the balls of my feet and unfolding my body into a standing position. From this new perspective, my circumstances are not as dire as they first seemed when I believed that there were only 2 options open to me. Either I would remain face down on the precipice eating gravel sandwiches or I would move and fall to my death over the edge of the precipice. I see now that there is another option available to me. This precipice is just a small part of what appears to be an endless expanse of orchards, fields, and grassy hills rolling in the distance. In front of me is a path lined with berry bushes leading away from the precipice.

Chapter Ten

"You don't have to have it all figured out to move forward." Roy T. Bennett

As this part of my story ends, I want to acknowledge the next steps. What's next? As we began on the precipice and now, we've moved our way through the period of desperation, 2% at a time, in these 10 chapters, we've reached a state of being 20% open to the possibility of change. That 20% moved us to the path leading off the precipice where we can move forward at our own pace and, if we choose, avail ourselves of the expansiveness of life's possibilities.

For now, I want you to trust that by just being open to being open you can move into a place of possibilities just as I have. The only requirement is a willingness to make a 2% change in your life. To begin to make changes in our life, all we need is a willingness to move in 2% increments past the fear of the unknown. By taking the first step of 2% and discovering that it is not in any way as scary as you thought it might be, you have opened your life up to what could be fantastic opportunities. You will no longer be face down on the precipice eating gravel sandwiches with no options.

This book is not a self-help book. It is a book that shares my trek from a life of utter desperation to a life of being open to possibilities. You and I are truly magnificent and as we continue to allow ourselves to be open, ANYTHING can indeed happen. Most of the things that happen when we're open are there to serve us.

As I said in the opening of my story, we each have our own agency and sovereignty and I bring this book to you as my personal journey. Your journey will be unique to you. This book is intended to be a guide not a prescription. I do not consider myself as an expert in anything. Please take from this book the things that work for you in your life and leave the rest.

This has been only a snapshot of a time and experience in my life along with the resulting insights that I received. Those insights direct my life as it continues to evolve and expand. My life is a work in progress - I practice being open every day and continue to learn. As a result of being in Rock Bottom I have gone from being someone who wanted to end my life to becoming a Life Enthusiast and I wish the same for you. Remember, you too can Rock The Bottom!!

Rock The Bottom

Rock The Bottom

Thanks

I am filled with gratitude for all of the specialists, alternative therapy practitioners, family, friends, acquaintances, spiritual thought leaders, happenstance meetings with strangers, and the new friends I met as I moved forward from my rock-bottom. My life would not be as rich without the contributions of each of these people.

As it says on the back of this book, I make no claim to being an author or a writer. My intention for this little book is to share the things I learned from my journey in the hope it may help someone who finds themself at their rock bottom.

My first rock-bottom was the stroke I had several years ago. It was close to my brain stem and left me with visual impairment and optical nerve damage. One of the results of that damage is that my eyes cannot view electronic screens for any extended period. In this digital age of communication using little screens, big screens and everything in between, I had to go "old school" to create this book. I dictated it and my generous mother typed, edited and formatted that dictation into this little book.

My old self would've proclaimed the multitude of limitations this lifelong visual disability brings with it. Instead, through the 2% incremental changes I have been able to make and continue to make, I now realize this disability is and has been my greatest teacher. It has gifted me, both literally and figuratively, with a new perspective and vision in life.

Rock The Bottom

About The Author

Andréa Vawda makes no claim to being an author and this may well be the only book she ever writes. She felt compelled to write it to share her Rock Bottom insights and messiness with you in the event you find yourself in a similar spot. Rock Bottom was a transformative invitation for her to live a greater life and she believes it can be that for you too.

Andréa is a former teacher, registered counselor, speaker and host who resides in British Columbia, Canada.

Manufactured by Amazon.ca
Bolton, ON